HITTING BELOW THE

FOR AMY —
WITH BEST WISHES!
JIMMY MARGULIES

EDITORIAL CARTOON COLLECTIONS FROM PELICAN

HITTING BELOW THE BELTWAY
The Best of Margulies

Jimmy Margulies
Foreword by Senator Bill Bradley

PELICAN PUBLISHING COMPANY
Gretna 1998

*For my wife, Martha, children, Elana and David,
and parents, Miriam and Henry Margulies*

---

*The word "Pelican" and the depiction of a pelican are trademarks
of Pelican Publishing Company, Inc.,
and are registered in the U.S. Patent and Trademark Office.*

Library of Congress Cataloging-in-Publication Data

Margulies, Jimmy.
    Hitting below the beltway / Jimmy Margulies ; foreword by Senator Bill Bradley.
      p.   cm.
    ISBN 1-56554-356-4 (pbk. : alk. paper)
    1. United States—Politics and government—1993- —Caricatures and cartoons.
2. New Jersey—Politics and government—1951- —Caricatures and cartoons. 3.
Editorial cartoons—New Jersey. 4. American wit and humor, Pictorial. I. Title.
E885.M368 1998
973.927'02'07–dc21
                                               98-14474
                                                 CIP

Manufactured in Canada

Published by Pelican Publishing Company, Inc.
P.O. Box 3110, Gretna, Louisiana 70054-3110

Contents

Foreword

Editorial cartoons have played an important role in American history. From the earliest days of our Republic, cartoonists have spoken out on the important issues of the day through their pens. The First Amendment protects these cartoons, which often discomfort the rich and powerful. They make us laugh, they move us to action, and sometimes, they make a real difference in people's lives.

As a New Jersey resident and a former United States senator, I am very familiar with Jimmy Margulies' work. He is simply one of the best in the business. Although he on occasion took me to task, I value both his ability and his insights into life in the public arena.

Jimmy is an asset to the media in New Jersey, and this book is a great display of his talent. Along with thousands of people in New Jersey and elsewhere, I look forward to seeing his work for years to come.

BILL BRADLEY

COLIN

SEMI-COLIN

Award Winners

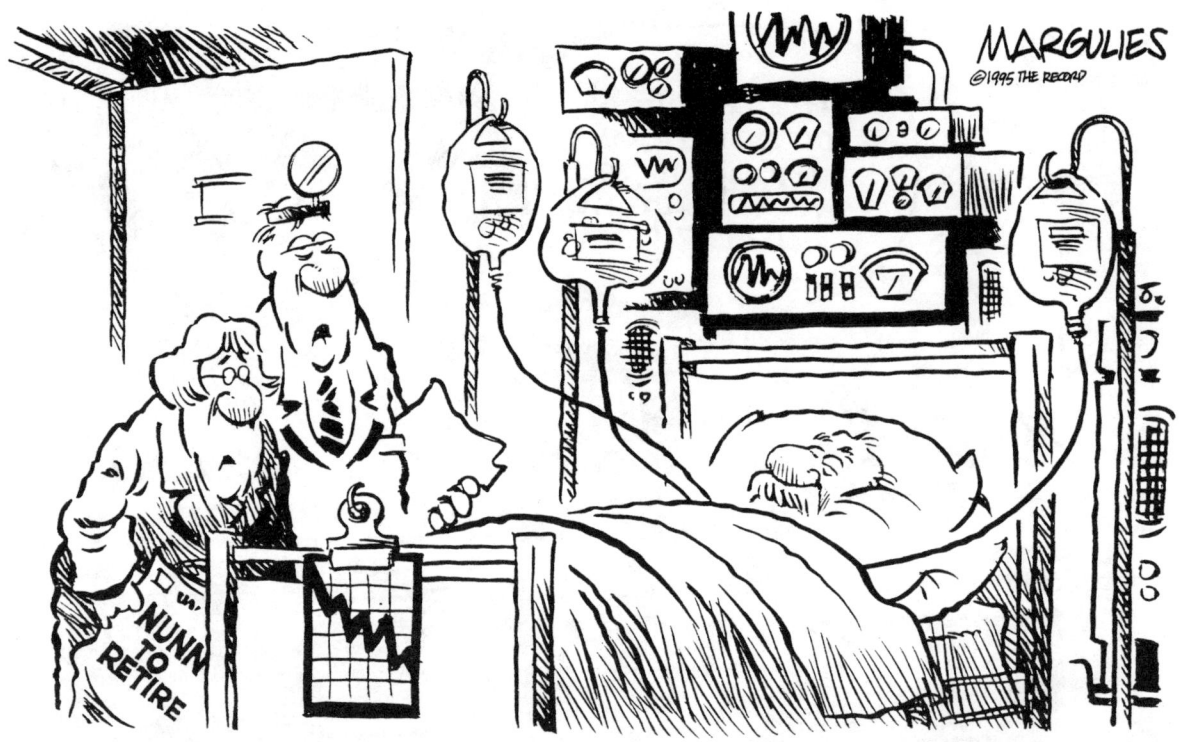

"It doesn't look good, ma'am...we've downgraded his condition from 'CRITICAL' to 'SENATE DEMOCRAT.'"

National and International

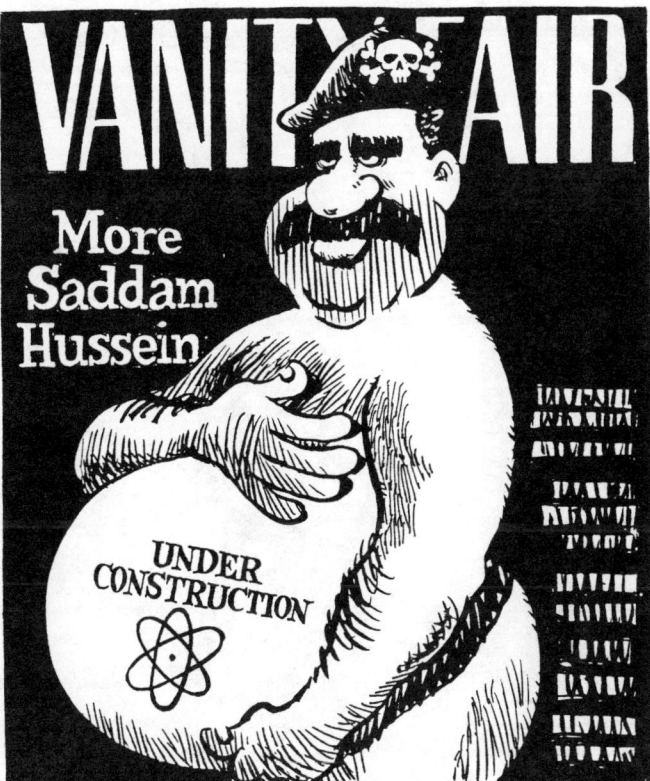

MARGULIES
©1991 THE RECORD
NEW JERSEY

COAST GUARD
REPATRIATION

MARGULIES
©1992 THE RECORD

Will the last Haitian to leave please turn out the light?

82nd AIRBORNE   **53**rd INFANTRY   **47**th EXPLANATION

MARGULIES
©1992 THE RECORD
NEW JERSEY

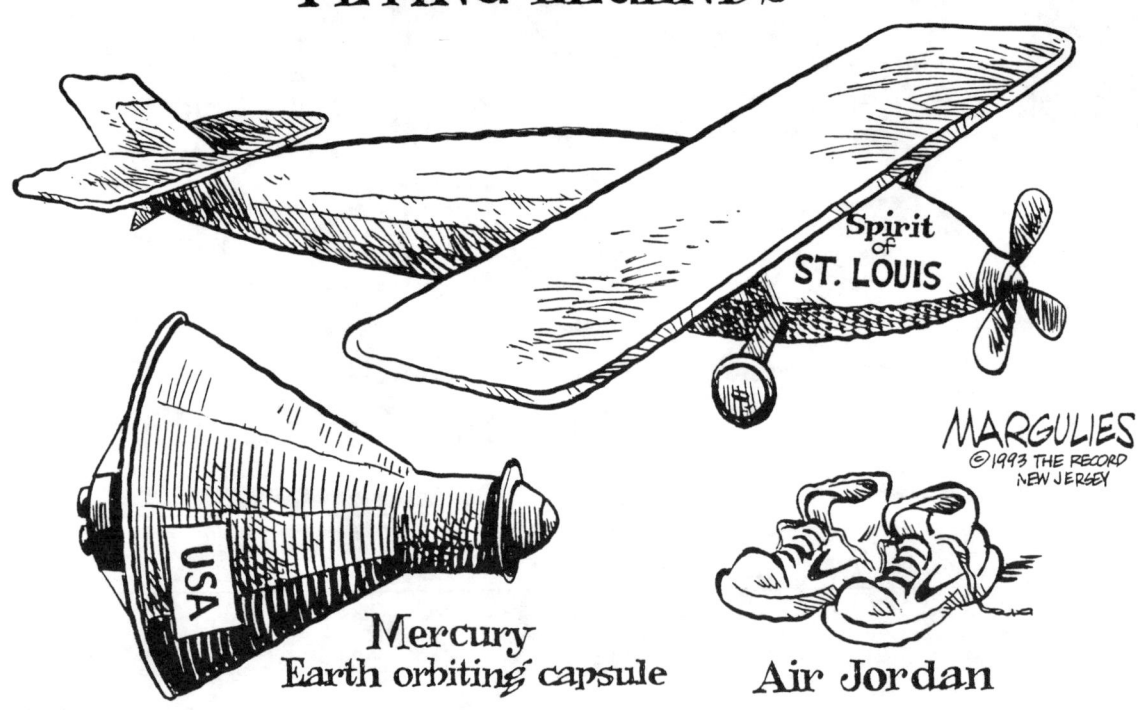

Smithsonian Air and Space Museum
FLYING LEGENDS

Spirit of ST. LOUIS

MARGULIES
©1993 THE RECORD
NEW JERSEY

USA

Mercury
Earth orbiting capsule

Air Jordan

WHICH TECHNOLOGY IS RESPONSIBLE FOR SKYROCKETING HEALTH CARE COSTS?

a.

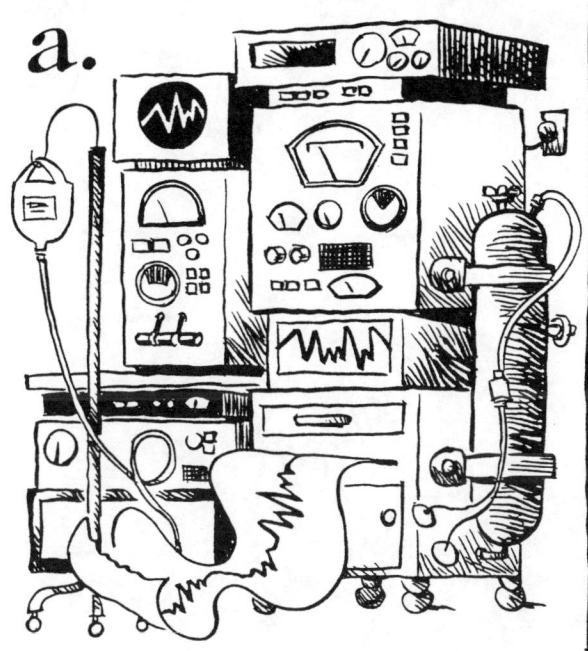

b.

MARGULIES
© 1993 THE RECORD

SERBS

ETHNIC CLEANSER

U.N.

MARGULIES
©1994 THE RECORD

"Hey, honey... *guess* what?...I still fit into my old uniform!..."

This child is
unvaccinated, unsupervised,
abused, ill-fed, and
never read-to.

What can he hope to become?

MARGULIES
© 1994 THE RECORD

Eligible for parole

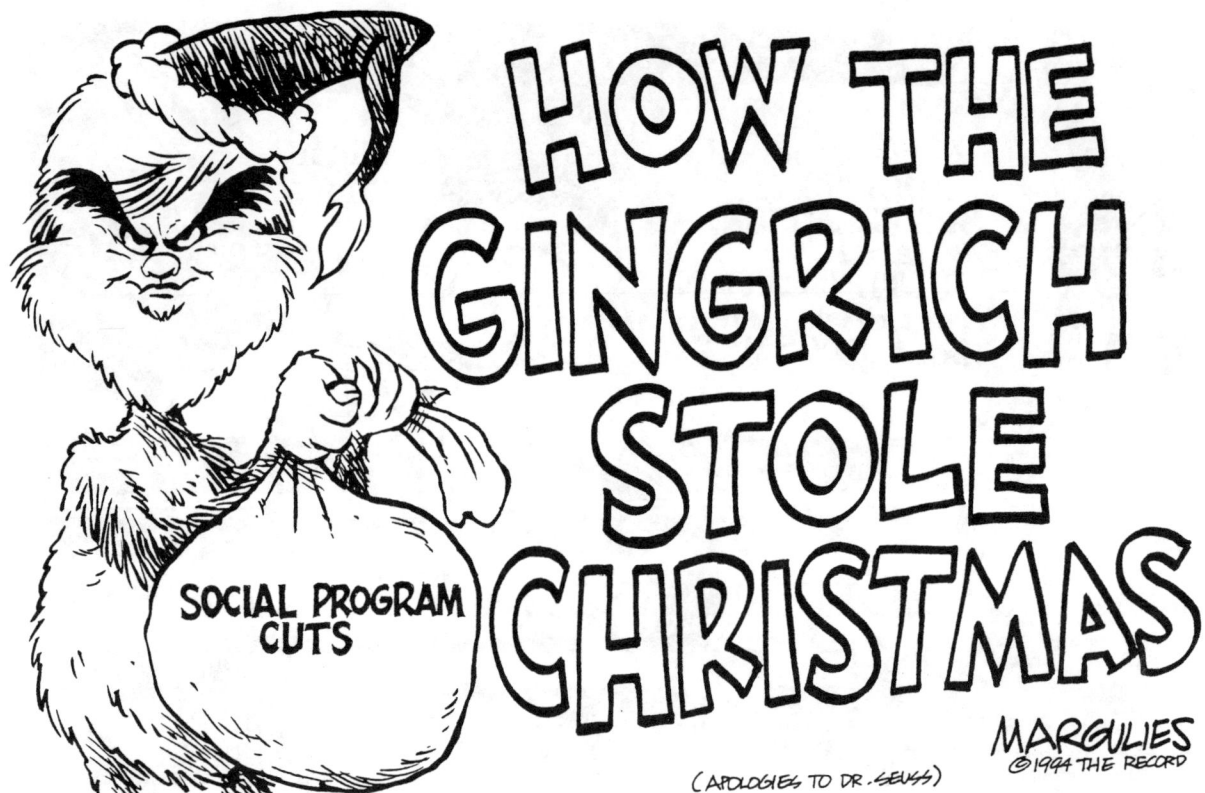

SOCIAL PROGRAM CUTS

HOW THE GINGRICH STOLE CHRISTMAS

(APOLOGIES TO DR. SEUSS)

MARGULIES
©1994 THE RECORD

"I hope you don't mind, Judge Ito... but testifying at the Simpson trial is the only way I can get the country to pay attention to what I have to say..."

"This makes it so easy to use a computer, even an adult can do it!..."

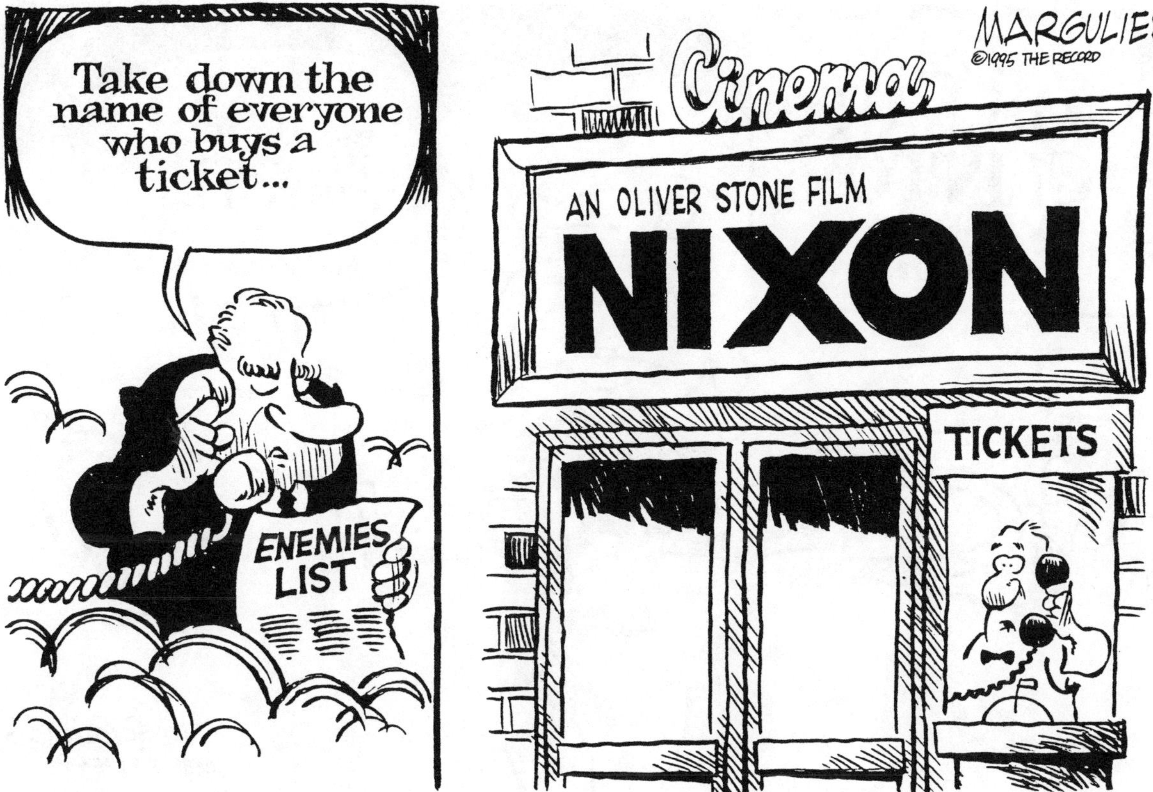

Ship of State

MARGULIES
© 1996 THE RECORD

Technological Breakthroughs:

Disposable employees

Disposable diapers

Luvs

Disposable cameras

MARGULIES
©1996 THE RECORD NEW JERSEY
JimMarg@aol.com

Montana

U.S. Commemoratives

32c

Jesse James
Father of Banking Reform

32c

Dr. Jack Kevorkian
Father of Health Care Reform

32c

Newt Gingrich
Father of Welfare Reform

MARGULIES
©1996 THE RECORD NEW JERSEY
JimMurg @ aol.com

★ MAPS ★
of the
CELEBRITIES'
SWEATSHOPS

MARGULIES
©1996 THE RECORD

"At least Congress is protecting us from same-sex marriage..."

WHY DO YOU WANT TO BE PRESIDENT?

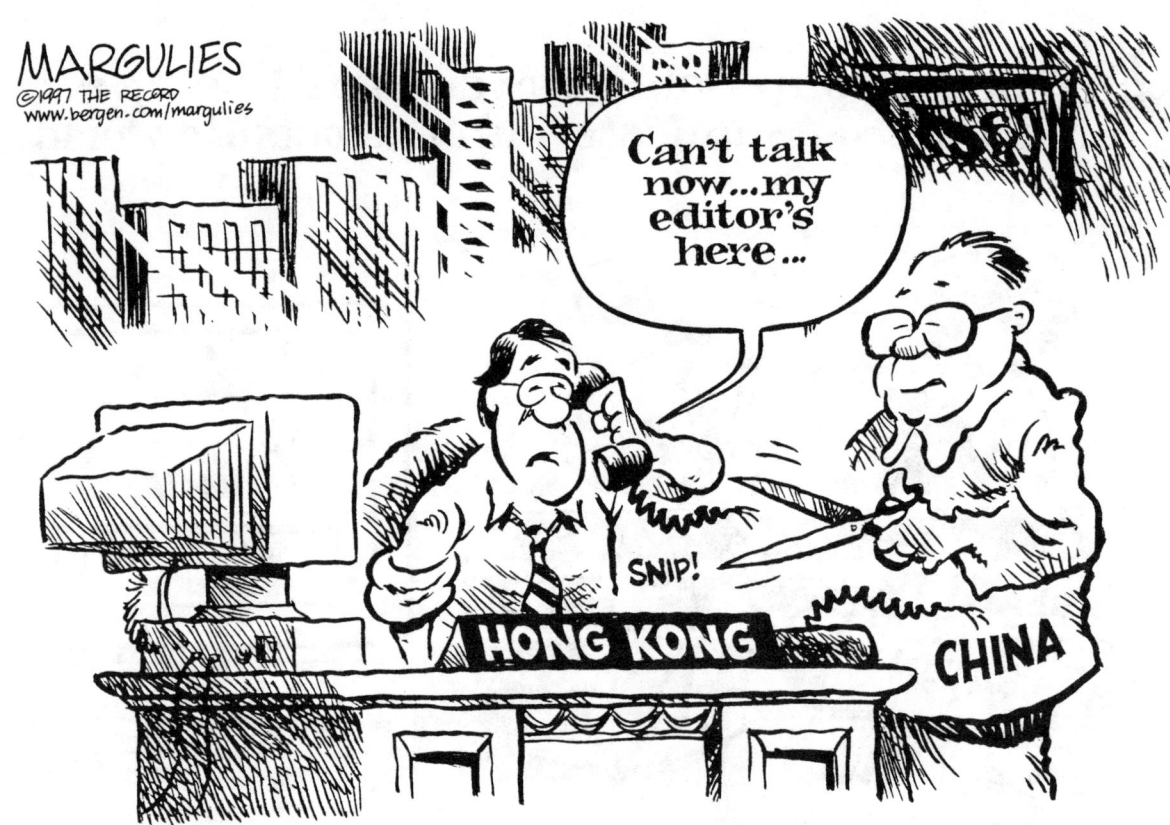

DUH!

Liggett Tobacco Co.

LIGGETT WARNING: Cigarettes are addictive and cause cancer. Tobacco companies lied about marketing to teenagers.

MARGULIES
©1997 THE RECORD
www.bergen.com/margulies

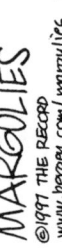

Then:

Now:

MARGULIES
©1997 THE RECORD, NEW JERSEY
www.bergen.com/margulies

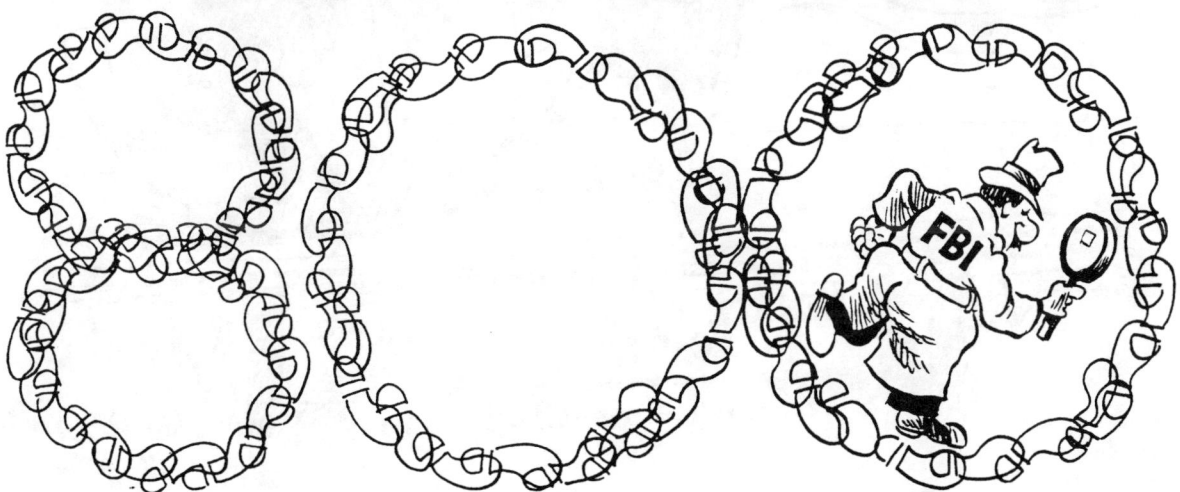

Federal Feeding Programs

FREE BREAKFAST

SCHOOL LUNCH

ALL-YOU-CAN-EAT BUFFET

ACCOUNTANTS

TAX LAWYERS

TAX CUTS

NEW FORMS

WRITE-OFFS

MORE COMPLEXITY

MARGULIES
©1997 THE RECORD
www.bergen.com/margulies

ATTORNEY GENERAL RENO INTERROGATES PRESIDENT CLINTON

New Jersey

RETURNS

N.J.

FLORIO

MARGULIES
©1990 THE RECORD

ASK THE HANDYMAN

Q. How do you stop a cesspool from overflowing?

A. Turn off the mike.

MEDIA

JEFFRIES

MARGULIES
©1991 THE RECORD

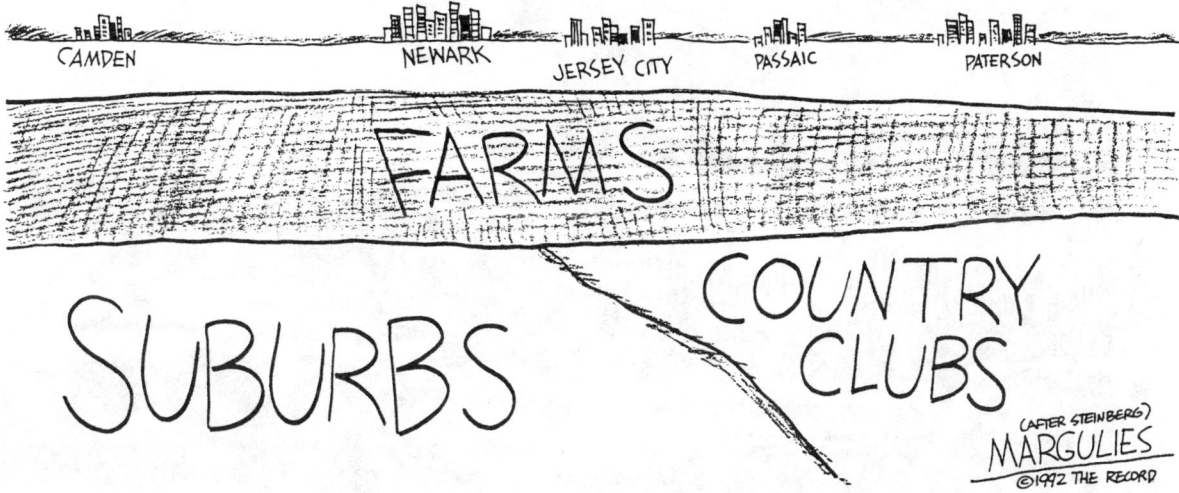

The Jersey TOMATO

The Jersey LEMON

SALEM 1
Nuclear Reactor

MARGULIES
©1996 THE RECORD
www.bergen.com/margulies

Governor Whitman wants to put the best face on her environmental cutbacks...

Better...

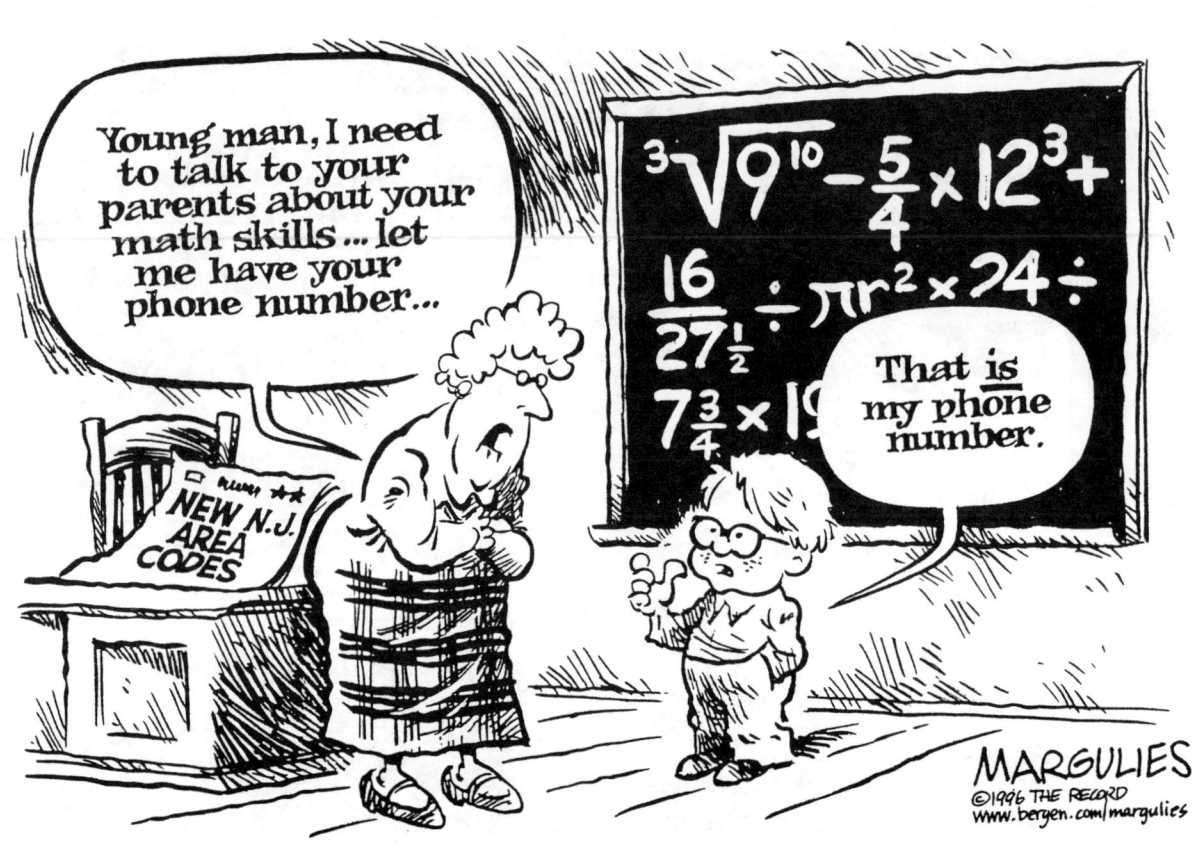

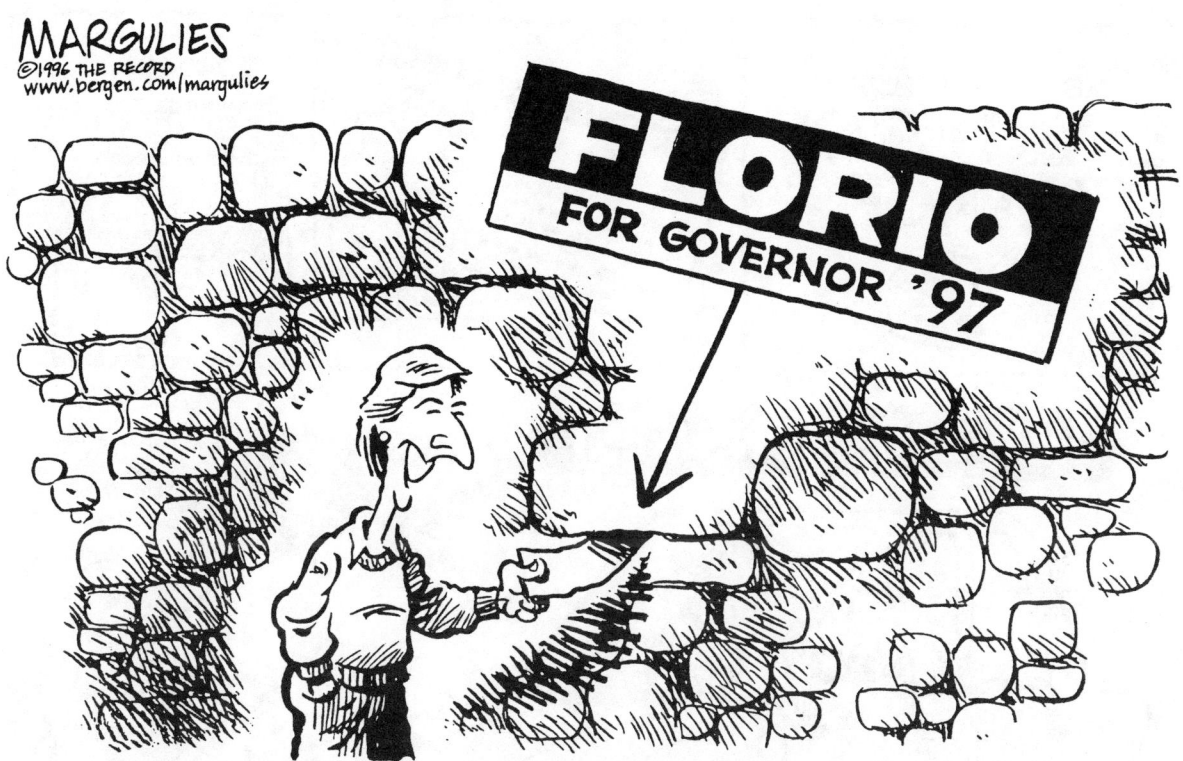

MARGULIES
©1996 THE RECORD
www.bergen.com/margulies

FLORIO
FOR GOVERNOR '97

Jerusalem: Governor Whitman slips a prayer into the Wailing Wall

New Jersey
GAMES OF CHANCE

DMV EMISSIONS TEST

MARGULIES
© 1997 THE RECORD
www.bergen.com/margulies

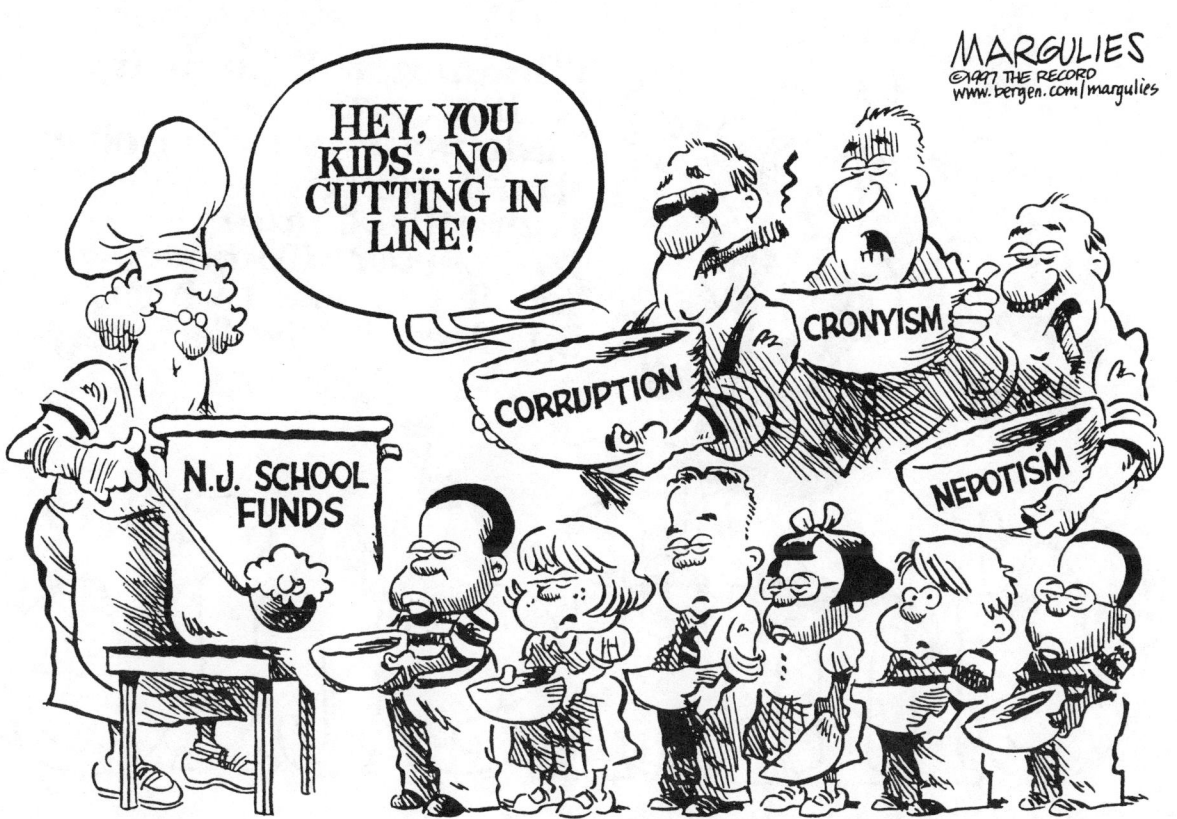

Dress Down Day

MARGULIES
©1997 THE RECORD
www.bergen.com/margulies

Banking

Law Office

State Government

About the Cartoonist

Jimmy Margulies joined *The Record* as editorial cartoonist in 1990. His work is distributed nationally to over 425 newspapers by King Features/North America Syndicate, and appears in *Time, Newsweek, Business Week,* the *New York Times,* the *Washington Post,* the *Los Angeles Times,* and *USA Today.* In 1996, he won two of the top prizes in his field, the National Headliner Award and the Fischetti Editorial Cartoon Competition. His cartoons on New Jersey issues appear in newspapers throughout the state.

From 1984 to 1990, Margulies was editorial cartoonist for the *Houston Post.* During that time he published his first collection of cartoons, *My Husband Is Not a Wimp!* In 1985, he won the Global Media Award of the Population Institute that included a two-week study tour of China. In 1990, *Ultra Magazine* named him to its list of Texans Who Made The Eighties.

Margulies began his editorial career with Journal Newspapers of Maryland and Virginia. A graduate of Carnegie Mellon University, he and his wife, Martha, a teacher, have two children, Elana and David.